Isolantie

Paari...

Isola road where Maija Isola used to live.

Maija Isola

art, fabric, marimekko

The story of a legendary designer of Marimekko

photo: Matti Saanio

Foreword

Maija Isola is the designer of *Unikko* – Marimekko's most celebrated print design. Maija created her first design in 1949, when Finland was rising up from the darkness of the Second World War.

Maija took part in a textile print competition as a student and her design work caught the eye of Armi Ratia, the founder of Marimekko, who took Maija's design into production. This fateful encounter with Armi allowed Maija's talent to come into full bloom. Maija created more than 500 print designs for Marimekko over the span of 40 years.

In her childhood, Maija loved being around her dear animals and in the nature. The vivid imagination she and her sisters developed while playing games would be an invaluable treasure and a creative resource in her later life. For Maija, freedom mattered more than anything else. Maija channeled the energy and love she experienced throughout her life into her work. The universal appeal of her work derives directly from her life. This book is a tribute to Maija Isola – the incredible boldness and character of her design.

Special thanks to Kristina and Emma Isola for offering valuable textiles and materials related to Maija Isola during the making of this book.

Contents

From a Marimekko catalogue.

JALKINEET
SKODON
akerros-
våningen

mann, Stockmanns' varuhus, Stockmanns', department store, Warenhaus Stockmann, Helsinki, Helsingfors Finland.

li Skanno, sisustusmyymälä, inredningsaffär, furnishings   Vilka Oy, huonekalutehdas, möbelfabrik, furniture factory, Möbelfabrik, N
op, Einrichtungsgeschäft, Helsinki, Helsingfors, Finland.

avila Fazer, Café, Helsinki, Helsingfors, Finland.

Above: *Omenankukkia*, April 13, 1977, Oil Painting,
Middle: Maija's mother, Toini, Eino I. Alitalo, 1969
Below: One of Maija's first paintings from 1946.
It adorns the wall of Kristina's studio.

Chapter 1

The beginning of Maija Isola's legend

Sources of inspiration

Left: Maija's mother, Toini and father, Mauno
Below: The house where Maija was born. It was built in 1919.

Three sisters of the Isola family: Tuulikki, Irma and Maija.

The Isola family

Maija Isola was born on March 15, 1927 in the village of Arolammi. The youngest of three sisters, she used to mention that her birthday was on the Ides of March, the date on which Julius Caesar was assassinated in 44 B.C. The idea for her name came from her father, who wanted to name her after his mother and grandmother. Maija's mother, Toini, was an active and modern person. She was open-minded and one of the first women in the village to wear her hair short. Maija always admired her father, Mauno Isola. He was an agronomist and had a talent for playing instruments, writing lyrics and composing poems. He wrote the lyrics of one of the most popular Christmas carols in Finland. The oldest daughter, Tuulikki, was fond of music and playing the piano. The second daughter, Irma, enjoyed writing, drawing and acting. For the Isola family, art was an important part of their daily life. They enjoyed reading poems when they celebrated a special occasion or exchanged gifts.

A natural childhood

The beautiful green fields around the family farm were a lifelong inspiration to Maija. Her rich imagination can be traced back to her childhood, when she spent countless hours exploring the surrounding nature. One of Maija's fondest memories was the day she encountered a big pike. She was lying down on a wooden bridge, gazing into a field ditch. In the streaming water appeared the head of a monstrous pike. The fish was so big that it seemed to go on forever. Maija was terrified and ran back home.

About freedom

While her sisters were at school, Maija spent a lot of time by herself. Already as a little girl, Maija felt that she could be free only if people took no notice of her. One day she ventured into the cattle shed in her new overalls. She fell into the manure gutter and ruined her overalls. Instead of running to her mother for help, Maija tried to clean the mess by jumping into the snow. This desire for personal freedom would carry through her entire life. Maija often talked about her own theory of freedom and the need to sometimes make mistakes. Her childhood experiences would eventually play a major role in her art and pattern designs.

Memories and animals

Maija loved telling stories about life on her family's farm. One Easter someone in her family set a plate of *mämmi*, a traditional Finnish Easter dessert, outside to cool. A cat walked into the yard and tasted the *mämmi* by putting its paw into the pan. Maija told no one about the curious cat because she was afraid that the *mämmi* would be thrown away. For Maija, Easter would be a disappointment without *mämmi*.

Growing up on a farm also meant that Maija acquired a deep affection for animals. As a child, she liked to pretend that she was a horse. To play along with her fantasy, Maija took to walking on all fours and ate peas softened in water and grain. She even prepared a place to sleep in the horse stall, but could not get her hands and feet to bend like a young colt. Not surprisingly, many of her designs were inspired by animal motifs, and the animal kingdom was always close to her heart.

Musta tamma, 1954

Mustasukkaiset hevoset, 1949

The Isola sister's dollhouse

The dollhouse

The Isola sisters were passionate about their paper doll game. In the 1920s, toys were not commonplace, so children used their imagination to invent original games. Every summer Irma and Maija were also supposed to help with the farm work. Their father wanted his daughters to set a good example. He taught them to shape perfect haystacks and meticulously rake the banks of the ditches. If the young girls did not succeed in their chores, they would have to do them all over again.

Maija and Irma worked hard on the farm, while Tuulikki, whose health was delicate, stayed at home and worked on the paper doll game, the main characters of which were teachers and office workers. Tuulikki used magazine pictures to make a dollhouse for the different dolls. She would later invite Irma and Maija to join the game as they were good at drawing.

Natural storytellers

After the younger sisters joined the game, the stories evolved in complexity and scale. They used recycled paper to make a fully furnished mansion, which had a wonderfully elaborate interior décor. Each room had portraits and beautifully detailed furniture. Exquisitely crafted, the dollhouses were something more than a children's pastime. The paper dolls with their highly expressive faces were given exotic names and clad in elegant dresses. Irma and Maija would plan the next twist and turn in the story as they worked in the field. These flights of fantasy helped pass the time and made working on the farm less arduous.

Even when their relatives visited on Sundays and holidays, the three sisters preferred to stay in the attic, where they could delve into their own imaginary world. They wrote down the characters' names, features, family trees and storylines in a black notebook, which became a cherished possession in the Isola family. The notebook also contained a detailed map of the characters' world,

with carefully drawn pictures of schools, post offices and stations. In another map, the sisters drew pictures of the surrounding lakes and mountains. The paper-doll game was a world separate from reality and a tribute to youthful fancy.

In 1949, when the sisters stopped playing the game, the paper dolls numbered in the several hundred. Later in her career as a designer, Maija would never struggle with boredom or creative indifference. Instead she often had so many ideas that it was difficult to choose which ones to work on. For Maija, these childhood games were not only a welcome relief from daily chores, but also a source of imagination and future inspiration.

A dollhouse made from paper. The incredible interior was created by the talented Isola sisters.

An accurate map of the paper
doll's world. The black notebook
contains explanations of the
characters and their stories.

Amfora, 1949

Left: *Amfora* published in the
design magazine *Kaunis Koti*.
Right: Armi Ratia, the founder
of Marimekko

Meeting Armi Ratia

Her first textile design

After graduating from elementary school, Maija moved to the nearby town of Riihimäki to attend upper secondary school. Her school work, however, suffered due to the ongoing war, and she often sold the food that was sent from home for hobbies such as watching German films. Living alone strengthened her sense of independence even more and led her to search for ways to live that were uniquely her own.

At the end of upper secondary school, Maija experienced major changes in her life. In the spring of 1945, when the Second World War came to an end, her beloved father passed away. On July 22, 1945 she married commercial artist Georg Leander and their daughter Kristina was born in January 1946. During that period, Maija thought about her career plans seriously. She had failed her final exams in foreign languages and mathematics and did not receive a matriculation certificate. Deep in her heart, she wanted to become an actress who overcame the hardships of life and achieved a freedom of thought and expression.

Through her sister, Irma, who was studying to be an art teacher, Maija met the artistic director of the Central School of Arts and Crafts, Arttu Brummer. He suggested that Maija should apply to the Central School of Arts and Crafts, as the school required no matriculation certificate. In August 1946, Maija moved to Helsinki to begin her studies at the school. It was so far one of the most momentous moments in her life as she departed from the family farm and animals she loved. Kristina was cared for by Maija's mother, Toini, which allowed Maija to concentrate on her studies. After the war, the general mood in Finland was that women should study and work. Toini also strongly believed that women should have an occupation. Although weaving was not her favorite subject at Central School of Arts and Crafts, she enjoyed drawing and painting immensely. To support herself, she was worked as a museum attendant. Arttu Brummer and Tapio Wirkkala were Maija's teachers, and she made friends with other legendary Finnish designers like Oiva Toikka.

In the summer of 1948, Maija travelled abroad for the first time. While working as a dishwasher in Norway, Maija visited the many museums of Oslo. She was fascinated by the Vincent van Gogh exhibition, the paintings of Edward Munch, and a collection of ancient pots and vases at the Norwegian Museum of Craft and Design. The print design *Amfora* was inspired by the museum pieces she had seen in Oslo. At that time, Maija also took part in the competition for printed fabrics at her school. Maija's works including *Amfora* caught the eye of Armi Ratia, who was starting up Printex Oy with her husband. The company would eventually become Marimekko. It marked the beginning of a lifelong partnership between the two women – a relationship that would produce some of the greatest masterpieces of modern textile design.

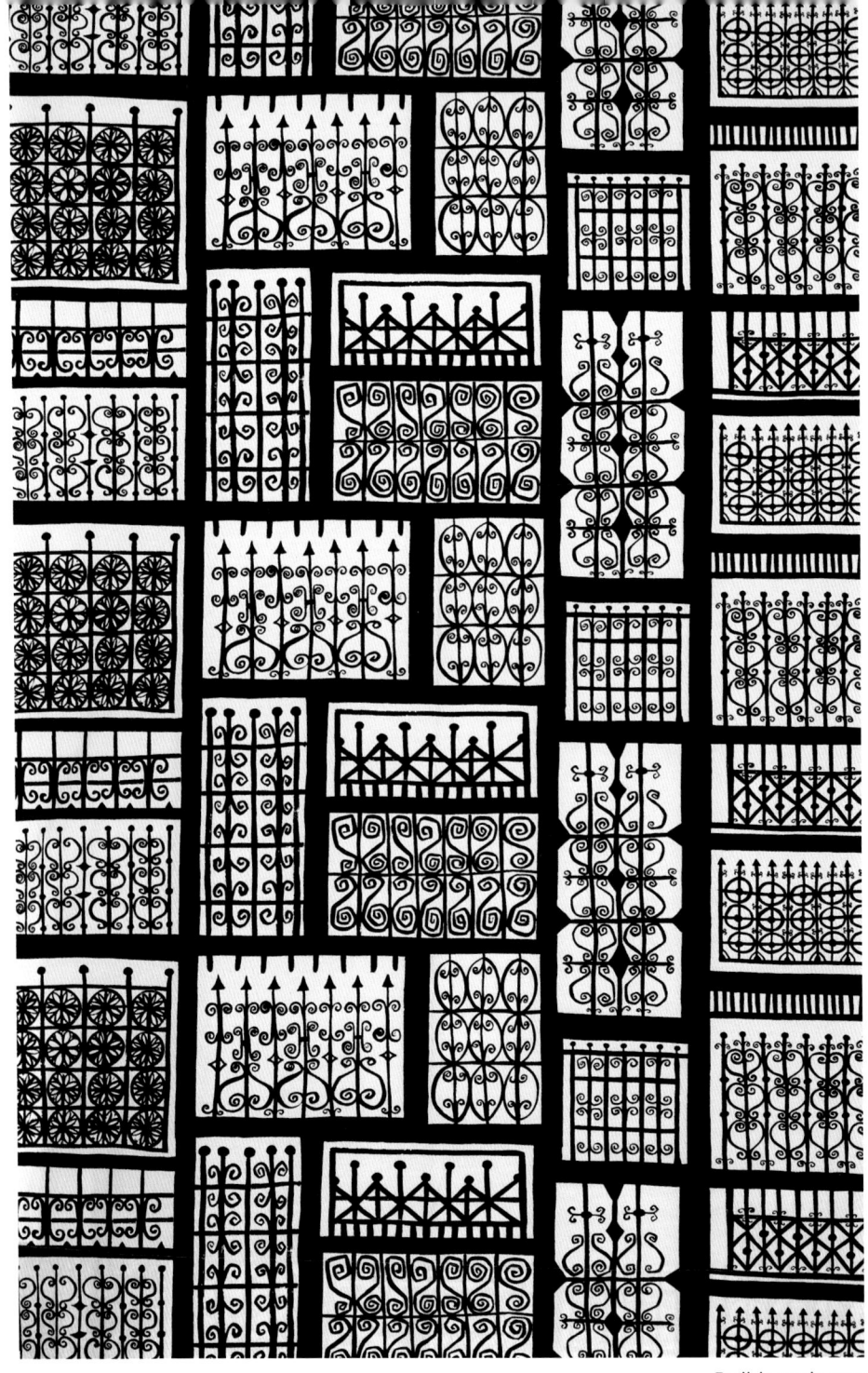

Pariisin portit, 1952

Kuningas, 1952

Norsut, 1952

Maija and Jaakko Somersalo in Paris at the beginning of the 1950s.

Painting and printmaking

Journeys with Jaska

The marriage between Maija and Georg was short-lived. In 1949 Maija began travelling around Europe with the painter Jaakko Somersalo or Jaska as he was known affectionately. They wanted to go out and experience the new world rather than settle down in a quaint house. Sometimes they hiked long distances, sleeping in the oddest places and cooking in the wild. According to Maija's letters, they took to the road like two gypsies. Maija wore clattering silver bracelets and a black velvet skirt that served as a sleeping bag. Their typical meal was called "Jaska's soup" – a stew made of meat stock, tomato puree, cayenne pepper and minced meat. Even though they had little money, they could rely on the kindness of others along the way. Travelling in Europe after the war was demanding, but Maija always looked happy when she talked about these trips.

During their travels, the two adventurers visited many museums and leafed through countless art books. Jaakko drew sketches he planned to sell in Finland. Through Jaakko, Maija learned new artistic methods like wood cut printing and her interest in painting blossomed. In 1953, Maija completed *Lunni* – a painting she had worked on secretly in Spain, while Jaska had been away. When they were together, Jaska was the the artist and Maija the assistant. After their divorce in 1955, Maija began to paint in earnest.

Printmaking in the 1950s

At the beginning of the 1950s, Maija often printed by hand on the floor of her dining room. She carved a pattern into pieces of rubber matting or wooden board and made printing blocks. Then she used a roller to spread ink on the block and printed on the fabric that was spread on a blanket. For printing, Maija used the tablecloths, sheets and plain woolen cloth that were leftover from the war effort. Recycled textiles were used as curtains and tablecloths at the Isola home and Tuulikki's house.

Maija also enjoyed working with crayons. Artists' materials were in short supply in Finland after the war, so crayons were a great discovery for Maija. She invented her own way to express the rich colors and beautiful texture of crayons. She first put thin sheets on a wooden board and then damped them. In this way, the colors became deeper and brighter than otherwise. Maija was also able to stencil the image directly. Print designs like *Iloa* and *Leppäkerttu* were created using the same technique. Despite the shortage in materials, Maija had successfully discovered her own signature style through trial and error.

Appelsiini, 1950

Iloa, 1950

Kivet

Several patterns designed by Maija were produced by Printex Oy in 1949. At the beginning of the 1950s, the collaboration between Printex Oy and Marimekko was not so active, which affected the number of designs Maija did for Marimekko. There were no records of patterns designs by Maija for Marimekko in 1951, '53 and '55. During these years, Maija was doing other jobs –for example, teaching fabric-printing classes at nursing homes and hospitals. It was in 1956 when the close partnership with Marimekko started, and Maija designed the *Kivet (Stones)*. The design was made from beautiful colored papers Maija had found. Simple round shapes made by scissors have great presence and form a continuous rhythm. It is still one of her most popular interior décor patterns. When Maija started her career as a designer, she made drafts for other designers in Marimekko. It was a valuable experience that helped her learn different printing techniques.

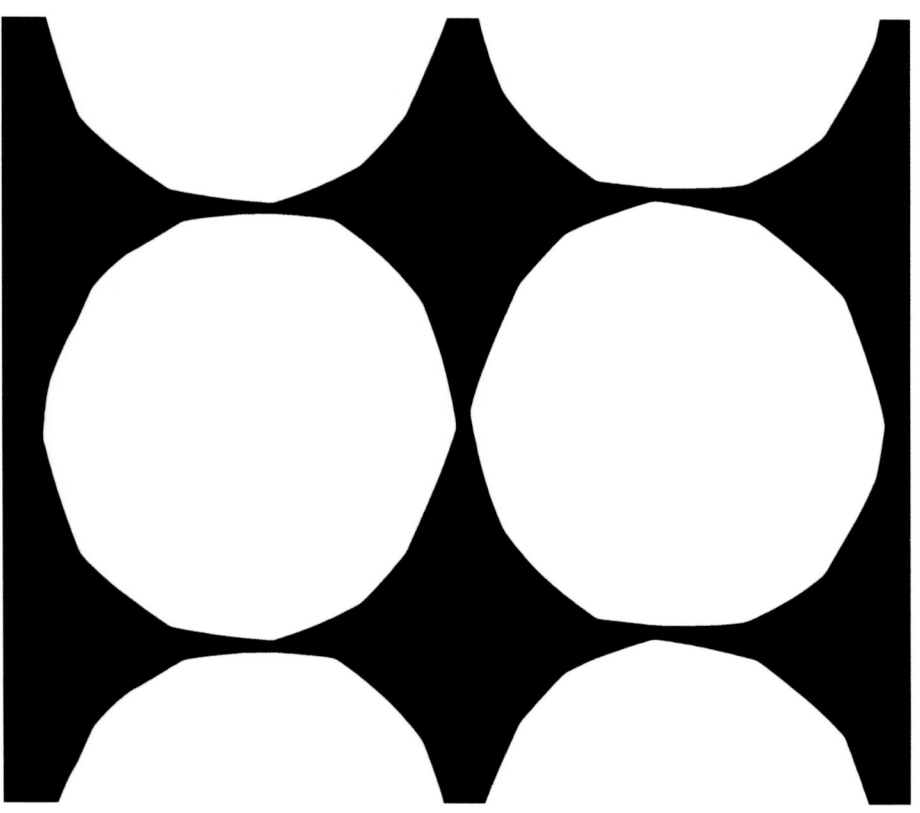

Isot Kivet, 1959

Luonto series

Until the middle of the 1950s, the patterns Maija designed for Marimekko were not necessarily related to each other. In 1957, she came up with an idea of presenting her designs as a series of patterns, and the first large series of works, *Luonto (Nature)* series, was created. Kristina spent her summer holidays at Maija's studio in Kaunismäki. She was eleven years old and was assigned summertime duties, which included collecting and pressing plants. Maija and Kristina worked together on the project on the sidewall of the studio. Collected plants were pressed between newspapers with a large cement block on the top. The *Luonto* series was inspired by Kristina's summer homework. Maija demonstrated an incredible ability to incorporate ordinary everyday events into her design.

Ruusupuu, 1957

A quest for method and expression

Maija wanted to use her daughter's pressed plants as images for textiles. She had to achieve her artistic vision with limited tools as there were no repro cameras or enlargers at Marimekko in those days. Maija went to the Marimekko factory in Helsinki by bus with dried plants that she had chosen as motifs. The plants were set on a suitably sized photosensitized stencil and then exposed. Using the small stencil, Maija printed images on a paper in one or two colors in order to make the final compositions. The final production stencil was made based on the final composition on the paper.

From 1957 to 1963, about 30 designs were created for the *Luonto* series. At first, only dried plants were used, but later Maija started to use fresh samples since she wanted to express the lushness of plants. Fresh material went bad so fast that Maija had to do the work as quickly as possible. Thick and juicy plants were difficult to handle. Using a little ingenuity, she sliced carrots into thin pieces in *Ryytimaa (herb garden)*. Maija's photogram-type of method was innovative to say the least. Besides minimizing the number of work stages, she was able to expose the plant directly to the stencil, which meant there was no need to buy expensive films. The overlapping of two colors succeeded in fading errors of alignment and unevenness caused by hand print.

Left : Kataja, 1962   Ryytimaa, 1957

Kahvila Tukholmassa, Café in Stockholm, Sweden.

...makylä Rantaloma, semesterby, holiday village, Urlaubsdorf, Joutsenlampi, Joutsa, Finland.

...intola ICA Stekhuset, restaurant, Gasthaus,
...rholmens centrum, Stockholm, Sweden.

Kahvila Helsingissä, Kafé i Helsingfors, Café in Helsinki, Finland.

Maija's designs were mainly used for the interior fabric.
From a Marimekko catalogue.

Ravintola Tawastin Kilta, restaurant, Gasthaus, Naantali, Nådendal, Finland.

Cafeteria, University of Houston, Houston Texas USA.

Colorful designs of the 1960s.
From a Marimekko catalogue.

Marimekko designs in the late 1960s, Game series etc.
From a Marimekko catalogue.

Tools and small objects belonging to Maija. She was fond of her possessions and held on to them for many years. Her favorite things were kept and used for a long time.

Chapter 2

Work. Travel. Life

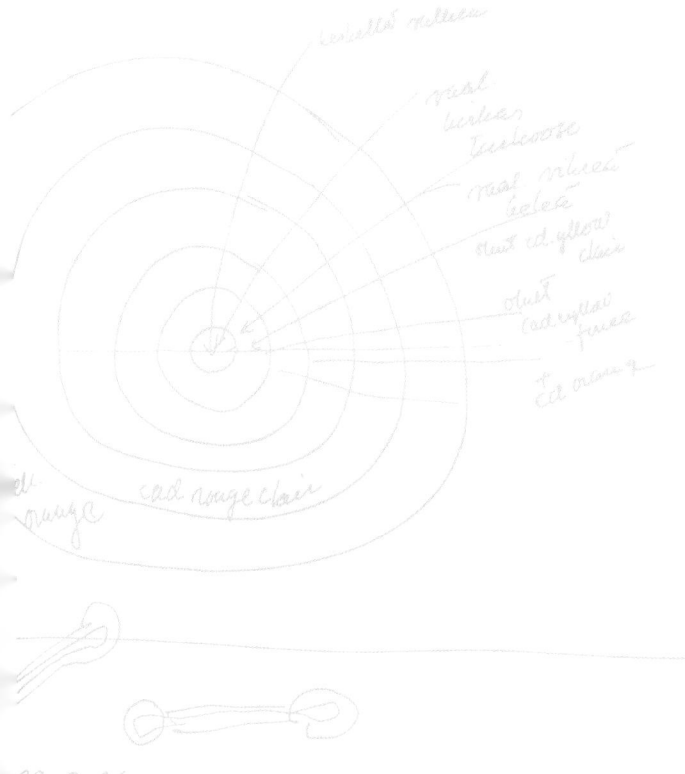

Road to success
. . . .

Ornamentti (ornament) **series**

Thanks to the great success of the *Ornamentti* series, Maija Isola became a celebrated textile designer. At the time, Finland was governed by President Urho Kekkonen and cultural exchange with the Soviet Union was active. Finns read Russian classics, enjoyed Russian films and listened to Russian popular music. Maija bought a book of Slovak folk art in Paris in 1958. She was interested in folk art and made a large series of print designs inspired by the book.

Maija painted a series of small sketches in the Slavic style of ornamentation on drawing films. This time around she decided to use an enlarger. The sketches were enlarged to the desired size. If the image did not fit the enlarger, it was cut into small pieces. Maija then made small stencils for printing and printed different compositions on the screen tables at the Marimekko factory. The process called for patience and precision. After considerable effort, Maija completed a variety of works, including small and large patterns. The series was first called *Bysantti (Byzantium)*. The name was later changed to *Ornamentti (Ornament)* series. The series contained about 30 works and most of them were designed between 1959 and 1960. The influence of Slavic folk art was visible, but the outcome was uniquely Maija - a novel combination of graphic line and enticing colors. Overprinting the rich colors and decorative patterns worked effectively and brought a welcome flourish to the designs. At the end of March 1960, the new collection was shown to the press and the colorful textiles were hung in the factory's printing room. Maija's work was highly appreciated by both the media and the public, which increased her fame as a textile designer.

46   Pyöryläinen, 1960   Right：Satula, 1960

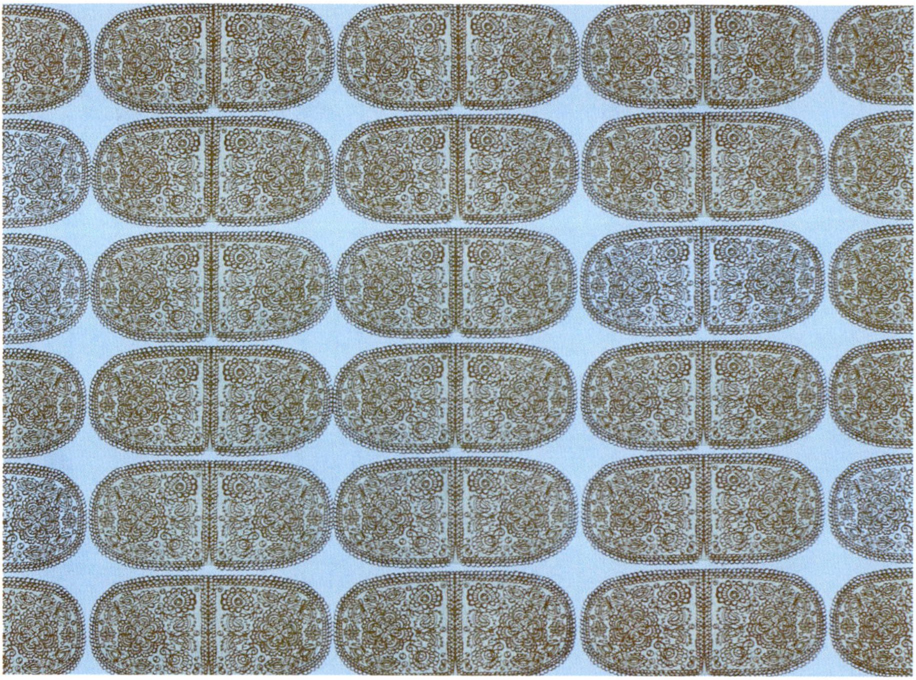

Tantsu, 1960

Sarafan, 1960

Savoijin kaali, 1962

Dombra, 1960

Joonas series

Around the same time as the *Ornamentti* series, Maija worked on the next series, *Joonas*. In this case, she preferred to sketch on a rolled piece of paper that was 1.5 meters wide and 10 meters long. She used a relatively large brush and gouache paints that had been bought in the Sennelier art supplies shop in Paris. Maija liked to draw patterns at home, but she was now forced to paint at the Marimekko factory in the evenings and at night because of the size of the paper. Maija also enjoyed painting to the music of Ravi Shankar. While painting, she felt as if she was dancing with her brush. The desire to experiment and live freely was reflected in the general mood of that period. Sometimes she finished dozens of meters of patterns in one evening. Armi Ratia chose which parts of the sketches would be used for fabric printing. It was possible to make printing stencils straight from sketches, which meant that the method was rather efficient from the standpoint of production. Unlike the intimate designs in the *Ornamentti* series, the *Joonas* series was almost monumental in size and visual impact. The distinct interplay of graphical and organic brush lines is characteristic of this series. *Joonas* (1961) continues to be a popular Marimekko print design.

Maija painting the *Joonas* series.

Nooa, 1961

Käki, 1961

Pannukakkua ja mansikkahilloa, 1964

At Maija's house in Kruununhaka. *Joonas* (left front) and *Nooa* (middle back) are used in the interior. The sketches for *Joonas* series were created at night in the factory. Photo: Arto Hallakorpi

Left : Joonas, 1961

LIFE OF MAIJA

Maija and Jorma

Maija's relationship with Jaska encouraged her to paint seriously. After their divorce, Maija devoted more and more time to painting. In 1959, Maija met Jorma Tissari, a judge and lawyer who greatly appreciated the arts. The couple soon married. At the beginning of the 1960s, Maija and Jorma left Munkkiniemi, a quiet residential area in the western part of Helsinki, to Kruununhaka in downtown Helsinki. In their Munkkiniemi home, they had a record player and antique furniture, but the apartment was too small for Maija's drawings. The new apartment was spacious and in good condition. Maija had enough room for enlarging and developing films and for making small stencils. There was even a large light table.

Up until then, Marimekko had paid Maija on an hourly basis. This minor grievance gradually affected Maija's relationship with Marimekko. For example, Maija requested a sofa for her workroom in the Marimekko factory as she could not relax on a chair. Maija got upset and quit the company because her request was turned down. She started working on her next print designs with her own equipment at home. Jorma had considerable experience solving legal disputes and helped mediate an understanding between Maija and Armi. Maija could continue her work at Marimekko with more freedom and independence.

Freedom

Maija often talked about the importance of freedom of behavior. When she was painting *Lunni*, her thoughts about freedom gained in intensity. Maija was a calm and quiet person by spirit, so when she spoke, her words contained a certain gravitas. If she was asked to talk about freedom, Maija would blush slightly and her voice would rise.

Mental freedom is a chance to do a job that you really want. The most inspiring thing is freedom. That you can do things by yourself on trips. Working alone at home, not in a factory.

Great mental freedom and no fools telling you that it won't sell. This style came from Armi Ratia. She was willing to try everything, and she always stayed that way. Everyone was given a chance, everything was experimented with. Marimekko: people liked each other, relationships were close. No burdening "family ties". Free. Mental freedom. The most important freedom is the freedom to fail, to mess up completely.(Maija Isola-Life, Art, Marimekko. Designmuseo, Helsinki 2005, page 4)

Lunni, 1953. Oil on canvas, 24x33cm.

Maija and Jorma got married in May 2, 1959.

Right : Silkkikuikka, 1961

Barokki series

The new contract was made and Maija worked on a new collection. The motif was European classic decorative patterns. Armi said, "You sold us the old wallpaper of *Seurahuone (Finnish traditional restaurant and hotel)*!" However, the traditional themes were expressed in simpler, more clear forms. The small-scale sketches were enlarged to the suitable size using graphical films. By adjusting the enlarger's aperture, exposure time and the film processing time, the appearance of the patterns could be changed. Maija bought an enlarger on her own and worked on these processes with her assistant, Ulla. She spent considerable time and effort in learning the entire process.

For Maija, exhibiting her new designs to Armi Ratia as ready-made draft films was always a significant event. The exhibition was usually held twice a year and the mood was often serious and opinionated. Maija guessed what Armi would buy in advance. The advantage was that print stencils used in production were made directly from the film, which helped streamline the production process. It was a significant risk to prepare the films in advance as there were no guarantees which patterns would be purchased. Some of the iconic designs in this series are *Ananas*, *Fandango*, *Savoijin kaali*, *Taskukello* and *Vanha valssi*.

Siniparta, 1962

Taskukello, 1962

Ananas, 1962

LIFE OF MAIJA

Life in the 1960s

In 1960, Kristina left her grandmother who had raised her and moved to Maija's apartment in Helsinki. Before then Maija and Kristina had often spent their summers together. They also met frequently during the winter months and exchanged letters when Maija was abroad. After Kristina moved to Helsinki, Maija and Kristina shared their daily lives. Maija was always working and never took time off for a holiday, so it was natural for Kristina to help her mother. Maija, Jorma, Kristina, Kristina's husband, Jorma's mother, and the family's many dogs lived in the same house in Kruunuhaka. It was an exceptional time in Maija's life and a wonderful opportunity to spend time with her family.

Maija and her dear Puska.

Grandmother

Maija became a grandmother at the age of 36 in January 1964. In the family, everyone was called by his or her nicknames, and nobody called Maija grandma. Maija was Baya or Abaya, and Kristina's nickname was Mille. Because of these nicknames, each person in the house had a unique role. Maija and Kristina also created the imaginary characters Ida and Räpi, both of whom showed up in daily conversations and letters. Thanks to them, difficult problems in everyday life were solved with humor. Maija and Kristina sometimes even received a surprise Christmas gift from Ida and Räpi. To Kristina, Toini was a mother, while Maija was a never-ending party. Maija and Kristina were very close and often mistaken for sisters. The relationship between the two changed over the years. When Kristina was small, she always adored Maija. Later Maija would become not only Kristina's close friend and teacher, but also her future work partner.

Kristina, Maija and Jules relaxing in Kaunismäki.

Armi and Marimekko

Maija had a profound respect for Armi and enjoyed working for Marimekko. Armi was fond of Maija's designs and trusted Maija's talent. Armi had a wonderful knack for marketing and business. She held an exhibition in the USA to promote Maija's designs. Maija received a letter from Armi in 1963. In the letter, Armi explained how Marimekko thrived on exceptional design work and how Maija's designs were indispensable to the company. The Marimekko spirit was frank and straightforward. Maija wanted to be independent and worked as a freelance designer for Marimekko. Sometimes she felt a huge pressure that she had to succeed every time, which made her want to travel somewhere far. Her passion towards her work was often intertwined with interesting places and personal relationships.

Maija as a designer

Maija enjoyed considerable success as a designer. Maija's teacher, Arttu Brummer, said to Maija that she was not particularly good at drawing, but still had the right attitude to be an artist. Maija was a passionate person who was strong both mentally and physically. When she was interested in something, she threw herself into it wholeheartedly. She was also highly imaginative and loved travelling. People tended to think that she was a bohemian, but she was a hard worker and always took a disciplined approach to her design work. Her studio was always clean and tidy. Kristina was also taught to take care of painting equipment as a child. For example, the tip of the painting brush should never be touched by fingers as this might ruin the brush. Maija was strong-willed and worked economically, but never took the easiest path. Behind every work was an idea or inspiration that drove her further.

Maijalle

THE GOTHA

Ne

Dear Maija,

olen ajatellutniita meidan asioita ja lopp
olkoon nyt miten paljon malleja tahansa ni
niita top hyviajokatapuksessa etta minakin
ja muilta en kankaita sitten niin haluakaa
linjat:

1) ihan vapaa hyva Maija print.   Nayttely

2) Marimekkoa ajatellen tehty Maija Print
   menna Printexsiinkin joka on sama ja yb
   vuoden perasta laillisestikin; Ensi job
   asia.

3) Nama vuoteenteljo asiat, lakanapussit j
   uoi joskus.Ajattelin ett. taytyy tilat
   gasta ja jattaa reunat valkoisiksi mut
   tunkea patjan alle. Mutta voiko neuloi
   vahingoittumista tai houryttaa. Kysy A

4. Tapetti.

Kyllahan tassa taytyy loytaa keinot; Lahd
kun tuntuu tekemiselta ja on hyva niin ai
keksin sen Siis itse asiassa ihan oikea
hyvan mallin ja sina taas teet niita aina
etta elat. Ja ateljeen voimme maksaa; Tam
koska emme ehtineet tavata, Oli vahan ki
keaa jai kirjeen varaan. Taalla nayttaa
kylla se siita.Tehdaan tanne Maija naytte
Ja suunnitellaan vahitellen -aivan rauhas
Tama etaisyys on hyva. Tulee aina vaan n

Hei hei voi hyvin

Sir GOTHAM   700 Fifth Avenue, N.Y. 19, N.Y., phone CIrcle 7-2200, cable Gotham, teletype

A letter to Maija written by Armi in New York City on October 25, 1963

Arkkitehti series

The *Arkkitehti (Architect)* series consists of different yet somewhat similar patterns. Armi and Marimekko wanted to use the series for marketing purposes. The fabric was designed to draw the attention of professional interior designers. The powerful graphical lines of the *Arkkitehti* series would be used to decorate large and open public spaces. Maija was against this idea. She thought that one should not think about the use of textiles when designing, but each individual should decide how to use the fabric according to his or her taste. Some of the iconic designs in this series are *Holvi, Kaivo, Karhunkukka, Kivet, Lokki, Maalaisruusu, Melooni, Pulloposti, Seireeni* and *Unikko*.

Kaivo, 1964

Right : Seireeni, 1964

Lokki, 1961

Melooni, 1963

"Forbidden flowers" 1964

Armi Ratia was adamant that flowers like roses should not be printed on textiles because they were at their most beautiful in real-life. As a decorative motif, they would not have the same impact. Maija detested rules and regulations, and she wanted to choose themes freely. In 1964 she made a series of floral patterns, which varied in composition from realistic to stylized interpretations. Armi changed her mind and ended up buying many of these designs. Among these floral patterns were *Karhunkukka, Maalaisruusu, Mehiläinen, Sukkanauha, Ruhtinatar, Vihkiruusu, Zinnia* and *Unikko*. The *Unikko* print design would become Marimekko's most celebrated pattern. Four of the patterns that were chosen by Armi had a rose motif. Patterns with plant motifs had been produced by Marimekko in the past, but this was the first time Marimekko came out with floral patterns.

It is impossible to talk about Marimekko without mentioning *Unikko*. The original drawing for *Unikko* no longer exists, but there is a painting with a similar motif. For Maija, painting was as important as design, with one influencing the other.

Right : Unikko, 1964

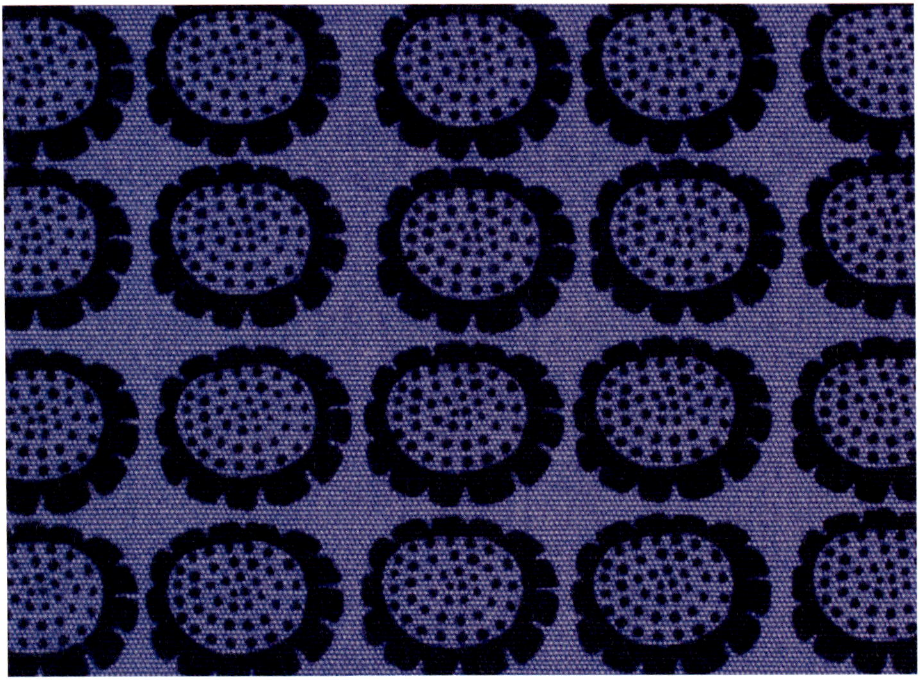

Mehiläinen, 1964

Ruhtinatar, 1964

Karhunkukka, 1964

Marimekko shop, Piironki, on Fabian
street in the center of Helsinki, 1964.
Piironki specialized in interior fabrics.
Photo: Design Museo

Right : Maalaisruusu, 1964

Vihkiruusu in a catalogue

Vihkiruusu (wedding rose) is one of those rose-inspired patterns. *Maalaisruusu (the country rose)* is a larger version of *Vihkiruusu*. These two designs were introduced at the beginning of 1960s, when the production of floral patterns began to blossom at Marimekko. After *Unikko*, *Vihkiruusu* is probably one of the most popular Marimekko print designs. In Japan, the pattern is sometimes seen in weddings. In 1978, a Marimekko Christmas catalogue featured multiple images of *Vihkiruusu*. Small color samples were included in the catalogue, with an accompanying description and illustration of each product. Lovely hand-drawn illustrations communicated the handmade feel of production in those days.

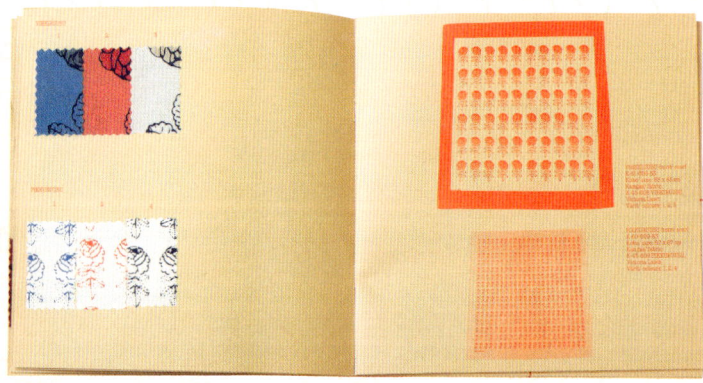

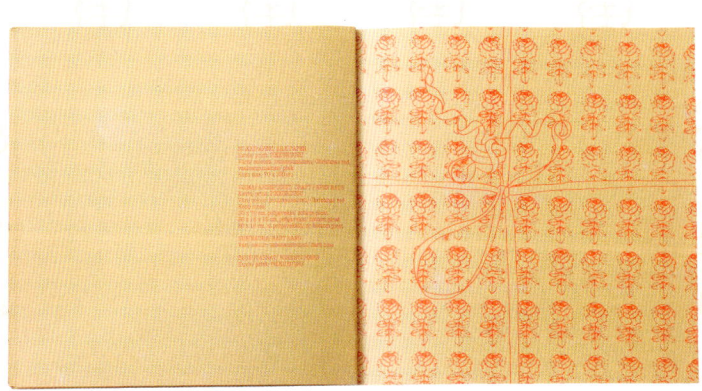

Sun and sea themes 1965 – 1967

Maija observed and took notes about the sun, sky and clouds. In these notes, she wrote down colors, color combinations, light phenomenon and afterimages from gazing at the sun. The same theme was repeatedly used in both paintings and print designs. For Maija, the sun was often the starting point for the composition of circles and ovals. When she visited Crete Island in 1965, she observed underwater life and the shapes formed by the movement of the water. During her trips, she made many sketches of the sea, and then completed a large sea-inspired drawing back in Finland. She brought seashells, which she set in front of the window at her home in Kaunismäki. This series includes the following designs: *Albatrossi, Meduusa, Osteri, Kaivo, Uimari, Viikuna, Villikaali, Pullopost*i and *Paprika*.

Meduusa, 1966

Simpukoita, 1967

Simpukoita 1967, Tempera on canvas, 87x130cm, Private collection. Photo: Markus Leppo

72

Villikaali, 1967

Villikaali, One of the designs related to the theme of the sun and the sea, 1967. Different colorways change the mood dramatically.

Siamilaissydämet, 1965

Pergola, 1965

Istuva härkä, 1966

Keisarinkruunu, 1966

Tuhat yötä, 1966

Juhannus, 1966

Florestan, 1976

Aurora, 1976

Peli series

Peli (Game) series was made in 1967. The patterns are inspired by colorful board games. Sketches were painted on paper that matched the size of actual game boards. The print designs were named after popular Finnish board games: *Kroketti, Musta Pekka, Pokeri, Ruletti, Hevosvaras* and *Merirosvo*. Maija also liked to play dice and cards. Winners would get sweets and coins. Maija was good at analyzing other players' reactions and body language.

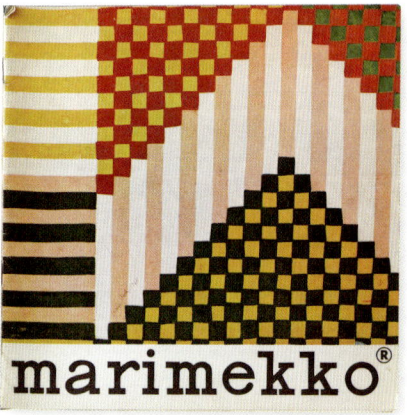

Maija liked to play games and was inspired by them. *Peli* series is of playful designs. Below: The numbers marked on the fabric indicate the order of printing screens.

Matti, 1968

Hevosvaras, 1968

Designs inspired by sun and sea themes and *Peli (game)* series.
From a Marimekko catalogue.

Catalogue

Pictures from a Marimekko catalogue.
Examples how to use the fabric in the interior are shown.

Maija's colorful and bold prints brought color to interior decor in Finland.

LIFE OF MAIJA

Life in Paris

In the late 1960s, Maija spent considerable time at the artist residence called Cité international des arts in Paris, painting and making print patterns. Her work was always the center and purpose of her life. If she could not work as freely as she wanted at home, she would change her surroundings. In this way, her life became simpler and she was no longer bothered by outside interference. Although she was not against having possessions, freedom and the independence were so important to her that even ordinary things and personal relationships could stress her out easily. The most important thing was to live as simply as possibly with only the basic necessities. Maija tried to stay away from the art world and politics.

Maija had a number of daily routines when she stayed in Paris. She painted, went to museums and department stores, walked around the city and in the parks, and watched movies. During these three-month stays, she sometimes watched dozens of movies. Through movies, she kept up with the latest interior design, fashion, music and ideology. In a letter from April 1967, she wrote that she found Marimekko clothes to be actually very nice. At first Maija was excited by the colorful clothes she saw in Paris, but after a while she preferred to see a more sophisticated use of colors. Eventually, she could not find anything like Marimekko in Paris and felt that Marimekko was full of surprises and variety.

In 1968, influenced by the student uprisings in Europe, Maija painted series of paintings with revolution as a theme. At the same time the subjects of many of her fabric prints from that period were also inspired by pop culture. These prints exhibited bold colors and contrasts, with motifs such as flowers, horses and strawberries. In the following year, Maija offered Marimekko thirty-one new designs, including the *Avaruus (Space)* series. These designs were influenced by pop art, and Maija also used this term to express her work. She spent the whole year in Finland. Maija and Kristina worked together more and more. They spent the summer in Kaunismäki and the winter in Helsinki. In the late summer of 1969, Toini, who had raised Maija and Kristina, passed away. That autumn Maija preferred to work by herself in the empty studio in Suomenlinna. She put herself in an empty space and concentrated on her work.

Maija painting on the floor.

Sketch of a pattern and Maija. Paris, 1970.

January 3, 1970 diary in Moscow

Why on earth must two people live together for their whole lives. I will no longer forget that I am blind, deaf and without emotions if I am not allowed to live alone. I mean the continuous knowledge of another person, which becomes so confused that one's psyche begins to blur. One feels it in the form of physical boredom and above all as mental confusion. (Maija Isola, life, art, Marimekko. Designmuseo, Helsinki 2005, page 76)

About marriage and relationships

Maija left for Paris again in the spring of 1970. She wanted to get away from the obligations of family life and marriage. She made her decision when she was listening to a concert of Shostakovich's Leningrad Symphony in Moscow during a New Year's trip. In September 1971, Maija and Jorma went their own separate ways. Maija and Kristina often discussed how they used human relationships as a catalyst for their work. Maija called this tendency "cannibalism" and stressed how falling in love gives a new perspective on an artistic work. Her feelings towards the men in her life were like a flame lit with devotion. Even though the impact of these men on her life carried over to her work, Maija always tried to keep her independence and freedom.

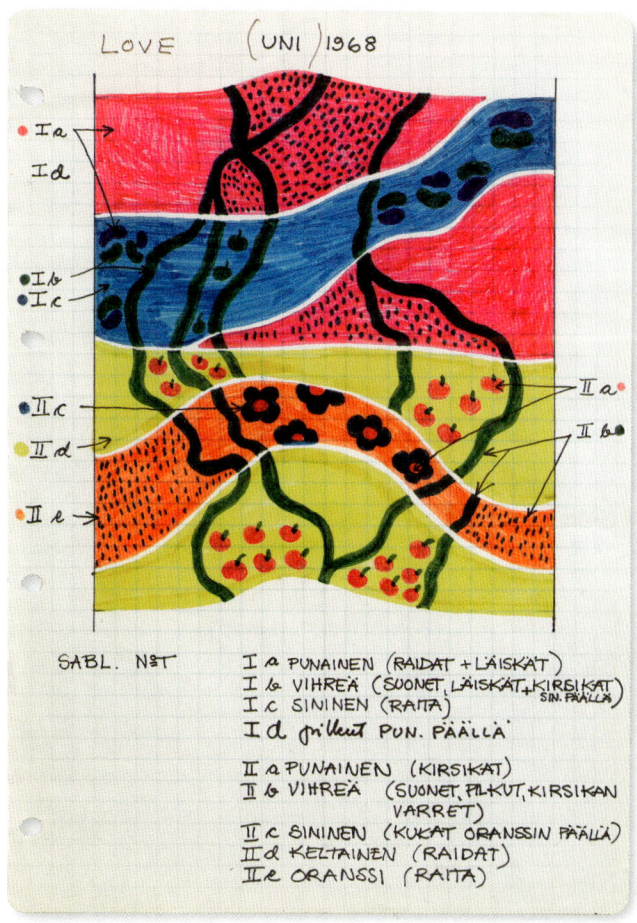

LOVE (UNI) 1968

• I a
I d
• I b
• I c
• II c
• II d
• II e
II a •
II b •

SABL. N²T

I a PUNAINEN (RAIDAT + LÄISKÄT)
I b VIHREÄ (SUONET, LÄISKÄT + KIRSIKAT SIN. PÄÄLLÄ)
I c SININEN (RAITA)
I d pilkut PUN. PÄÄLLÄ

II a PUNAINEN (KIRSIKAT)
II b VIHREÄ (SUONET, PILKUT, KIRSIKAN VARRET)
II c SININEN (KUKAT ORANSSIN PÄÄLLÄ)
II d KELTAINEN (RAIDAT)
II e ORANSSI (RAITA)

Archive

Maija's designs were already being reproduced during her lifetime. To make her work easier, she kept accurate information on individual print patterns. The depository of this information became known as the "pattern books." These books contain color sketches of one repeat drawn in a smaller scale, the size of the repeat, and printing orders. They are still in use and serve as an essential manual to ensure that the reproduced pattern is as faithful to the original design as Maija intended.

Left : Lovelovelove, 1968

Color samples of *Max ja Moritz* (1968). The design is inspired by a darkly humorous German tale from 1865.

Colors

For her new designs, Maija carried out test prints in original colors first and then in black and white. In this way, she obtained the desired screens and saw how colors with strong contrasts affected the patterns. According to the many color swatches, Maija experimented repeatedly before she found the ideal color combination. A great number of color tests were performed in the 1960s and 1970s. Sometimes up to fifty tests were done for one pattern. At that time color charts like Pantone did not exist, so Maija created her own color charts. She mixed the desired hue in gouache before painting. Then she showed it to Marimekko's paint workshop. Maija had an amazing eye for color.

Left : Max ja Moritz, 1968

Mansikkavuoret, 1969

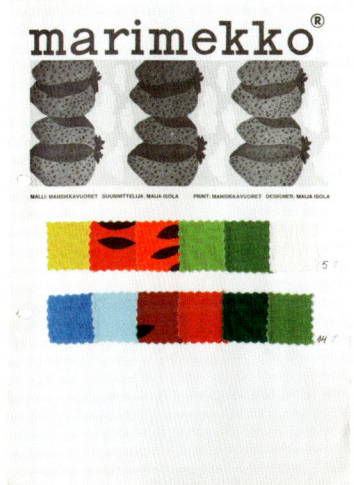

Above: pattern book for *Mansikkavuoret* (1969).
Below: various color samples.

Ibir, 1970

Onnea, 1970

Pepe, 1970

Päärynä, 1969

Sitra, 1968

Ofelia, 1968

Several colorways were made for this pattern. The fabric was named after a character in *Hamlet* by Shakespeare.

04

LIFE OF MAIJA

Her favorite things

Unlike the strong and bright colors used in print design, Maija liked rather soft and tranquil colors for the interior of her home. The paintings on her walls were often rich in color, though could also be painted in a solid monochrome. She preferred white, black and other dark color schemes in her house. Later in her life, she liked to use her favorite colors: light blue and light pink. The wall of the studio was painted in white tones. For the color combination in her print design *Fandango*, Maija especially chose colors she wanted to use at home. In Algeria, she used *Fandango* of the blue plum-fuchsia colorway. Maija loved cushions and owned cushions of different sizes, colors and materials. Some of the furniture and objects that were close to Maija's heart stayed with her throughout her life. The sturdy office furniture she inherited from her father, two armchairs and a sofa, were well taken care of and their upholstery was redone several times. A sledge coverlet of brown sheepskin and moss-green broadcloth were used until they were threadbare. Favorite objects were displayed in a special place: two small wooden horses, her father's shaving cup, butter casks, milk jugs, and a coffee pot. She could not depart with them because each object was full of memories. Maija also liked kitschy objects like a Japanese piggy bank in the shape of a beckoning cat. One of Maija's favorite possessions was a black-covered notebook with red corners, which she later developed into a scarf design.

kani ja tulppaani, 1968

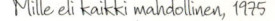

Mille eli kaikki mahdollinen, 1975

Mille eli kaikki mahdollinen, gouache 130x273cm. The story of Kristina moving to the countryside in the early 1970s. Private collection. Photo: Markus Leppo

Inspired by Ahmed

In 1970 Maija visits Paris yet again. During this trip, Maija met Dr Ahmed Al-Haggagi who was an Egyptian scholar of Islamic theater. Their friendship gradually evolved into a love affair. Ahmed's influence can be seen most prominently in the print designs *Kuningatar, Naamio, Poppy, Sadunkertoja* and *Tumma,* with many of themes inspired by Arab and Egyptian culture. Ahmed drew his ideas on a small piece of paper and Maija would then create a large-scale painting of the idea on a piece of rolling paper. Ahmed was impressed with how quickly Maija turned his pencil and pen sketches into large and colorful paintings.

Sketch of Ahmed

Poppy, 1970

One of several works by Maija inspired by Ahmed's sketches.

Välly, 1972

Välly is a sleigh covering. Right: the real-size painting made on a paper of 150cm width.

Animal kingdom

Since she was a child, Maija loved animals. In her childhood she grew up with horses and cows at the farm in the countryside, and she lived her life surrounded by animals even as an adult. She had dogs in Helsinki and many animals in Algeria – a stray dog called Laika, a brown Arabian hen, two rabbits called Robin and Lulu, two doves and two tortoises. Animals became a favorite motif in her paintings and print design. In 1970, she found a wonderful book about animals in Paris and made a painting of a leopard inspired by the book. She would later use the same motif in her print design *Kaksoset*. Maija felt that she could relax in the presence of animals and always found inspiration in them.

Paris sleeping jaguars, 1976

Kaksoset, 1970

Kaksoset 1970, gouache on paper
68x150cm, Private collection.
Photo: Markus Leppo

Kaksoset, 1970

Gouache on paper, Ain-El-Turc, 1972.
A painting of a small village in Algeria.

Maija mixed her own colors
as well as prepared her own
color charts for paintings.
The color on the left is
named Algeria.

05

LIFE OF MAIJA

Algerian dream

In the spring of 1971, Maija went to Paris and left for Ain-El-Turc, Algeria with her artist friend. With help from their friends, she rented a villa with a sea view. In the yard, there were date palms, grapevines, roses, and many unfamiliar plants. The mood in Algeria was poetic: ramshackle houses, the white light of the sun, a park in dim light, and a multitude of people. Maija felt comfortable there, because the land reminded her of places she had dreamt of. Everything was so different from Finland. She enjoyed living in Algeria immensely and wrote in her diary that she felt as if she were in heaven. Maija became friends with Casimir and Muhamed. They had an unforgettable time together, on the beach, at the villa, and on picnics in the mountains. Maija even received a hen as New Year's gift from Muhamed, but didn't know what to do with it because she was less than passionate about domestic fowl.

When Maija talked with foreigners, she spoke a mixture of languages. Her lingua franca included languages she had learnt at school such as Swedish, German and Latin and what she studied during her trips such as French, Spanish, Italian and English. The people around Maija soon got used to her unique way to express herself.

From 1971 to 1974, Maija had to leave Algeria every three months to renew her residence permit. Her time in Algeria was one of the most dramatic periods in her life. She experienced an ideal way of life, full of happiness and bitter disappointment. She felt as if she found the most suitable place for living and making art. Sometimes she had a hard time understanding the difference in cultures and the role of women in an Islamic society. Muhamed had a fiancé, but Maija could not stop loving him even if she felt utterly helpless at times. She was shocked when Mohamed married his fiancé. The quarrels surrounding Muhamed's decision would eventually persuade Maija to leave Algeria.

Kukkamaljakko ja meri, 1971

Kukkamaljakko ja meri 1971, gouache on
paper, 154 x 144. The influence of Islamic
ornamentation is visible.

Teekannu, 1972

Teekannu 1972, oil on canvas,100 x 100, Algeria. The combination of the side-curtain and the pot creates a mysterious space.

Tori, 1970

Häälaulu, 1971

Charles, 1973

Left : Tuuli, 1971

Manteli, 1974

Spring in Paris, 1976

In 1970, Maija met Ahmed Al-Haggagi, an Egyptian scholar. They kept in touch over the years, exchanging letters and meeting occasionally. After Maija left Algeria, the contact between the two increased. In early 1976, Maija had an opportunity to work with Ahmed and created several print designs inspired by Egypt: *Feria, Niili, Nubia, Narcissos* and *Papyrus*. She stayed in Paris for three months and worked on paintings of flowers. Among these works are *Come near me, Kiss me or love me more*, and *Spring*. As indicated by the titles, she seemed to be experiencing a blissful moment in her life. In her diary, she wrote how happy she was in Paris, bothered neither by the past nor the future. She could do what came to her mind.

Made on March 16, 1976, when Maija celebrated her 49th birthday, this painting would later become the fabric pattern *Kohtaaminen*.

Kohtaaminen, 1976

fallah, 1976

Come near me, 1976

spring, 1976

Kiss me or love me too much, 1976

Niili, 1976

Nurmikko, 1976

Dyyni, 1983

Dyyni (Dune), 1983. The big compass purchased from an art supply shop was used for this design. Left: the original sketch of the design.

Paprika, 1965

Left: Original sketch of *Paprika* (1965). *Pulloposti* is a larger design of the same motif. *Paprika* also is the Finnish word for bell pepper. In the 1960s, bell peppers were still an uncommon vegetable in Finland.

Sketchbook

Robin

KUKKATORI

orange

jaune

jaune

rouge

typien   vaal.   vaal raidat
                              Ty.

vaal.

Orange   vaal.   typien

vaal. prun vt. prun

ANSAR ASA   WYNN LOHDUTUS

UR VISENTTI   KEN SOIHTU

...ynyt, joten korvat ovat kiinostuneet, nenä kerä röityNyt ja silmät suuret. Täällä Torttilan pihassa kasvaa paljon koivuja tasaisella pihamaalla joka on laaja ja nurmettunut. Vanha päärakennus ja uusi talo jossa Aija, Hannu, Heikki ja Eva asuvat, ovat toisiaan vastapäätä ja niiden välissä kellimittain on suuri tiilinavetta. Hannulla on aivan kiltteä pieni metsästys- koira Viima. Se on virkeä, tarkkaa vainen ja kova nuuskimaan. Kirkea vikkikoira. Pohja- väri on valkea mutta siinä on ruskeita laikkuja ja jotain mustakin täikkiä. Hannu käy sen kanssa metsällä. Metsästää jäniksiä ja kettuja. Täällä on myös kaksi mustaa ponia tallissa. Toisen nimi on Pikku

17.3.90

Laika·Laika·Laika.

Cin katto

The family tree of the Isola family by Emma, Maija's granddaughter, 2010.

Chapter 3

Maija's late years, and legacy

A new departure

Life in the USA

Ahmed was a lecturer at University in Boone, North Carolina and Maija decided to try living there for one year in the spring of 1977. One of the purposes was to search for opportunities to work as a textile artist in the US. However, it was difficult to sell her designs since there were few factories specializing in Maija's type of print fabric in the USA. Maija enjoyed the small-town lifestyle. She was attracted to the forest that was different from the Finnish forest and especially liked the big silvery oak trees. While there, she was always coming up with new ideas for paintings. The time in Boone passed peacefully, with leisurely walks in the mountains and practicing yoga. Maija gathered plants to be used as design motifs, and was highly motivated to work on paintings about the Appalachian Mountains. Maija used to say that Boone reminded her of her hometown, Riihimäki.

In Boone, 1977.

Indian dance, 1977

Madison, Wisconsin. July 18, 1977.

Mansikkamaito, 1979

Niitty, 1979

En malttaisi syödä
aamiaista
Tänään lähdetään maalle

Jag vill inte äta just nu
I'dag far vi till landet

I'm too excited to eat
breakfast. Today we
leave for the country

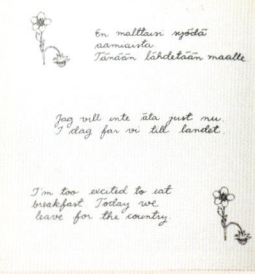

Leenalla on nimipäivät.
Minä annan lahjaksi man-
sikkahelmän. Äiti leipoo pii-
rakan.

Leena har namnsdag. Jag ger
henne ett smultronband i gåva.
Mor bakar en piråg.

It's Leena's name day.
I'm going to give her
wild strawberries strung
on a stalk of grass.
Mother is baking a pie.

Pannwagen vieressä on pyykki-
naru. Kun äiti ripus-
taa pyykkiä, istun va-
jan edessä. Näin minä
kerran sisiliskon.

Nära vedlidret är snäret ett byk-
snöre. När mor hänger upp byke
sitter jag framför lidret en gäng
såg jag där en ödla.

There's a clothesline next
to the woodshed. I sit
beside the shed while
Mother hangs up the
laundry. I saw a
lizard there once.

138

Strawberry girl catalogue

In 1979, Maija created a print design with wild strawberries as the lead motif. In the forest around Kaunismäki, there were plenty of small and sweet wild strawberries every year. For Maija, the inspiration for print designs often lurked in the surrounding nature. The homemade catalogue was made by the Isola family, based on this lovely print created from a child's perspective. Kristina was in charge of planning, making beautiful berry pies, writing stories and designing the catalogue's artwork. The models were Kristina's children, Jaakko and Emma, and their father Markus Leppo was the photographer. Emma was wearing a dress made by Kristina. It was Emma's favorite summer dress. The photo shoot took place near their house in Riihimäki and the finished catalogue was as sweet as a wild strawberry.

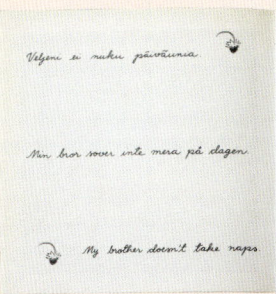

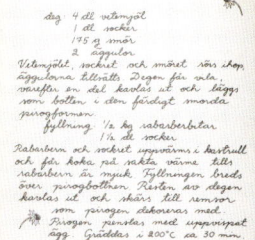

New Era – two designers

During her stay in the USA, Maija read the works of philosophers like Plato, Thoreau and Emerson. She read them out loud in the evening while at the same time recording them on to a cassette tape. She would then listen to the recordings while working. It was easier for Maija to understand texts this way. In 1977, the theme of her designs for Marimekko was minimalistic and meditative. The following year, the collaboration with Marimekko seemed to have ended. Maija discussed with Kristina if she should continue working for Marimekko and asked Kristina if she could work with her as a print designer. At that point Maija and Kristina began to work together as a duo and both names were printed on the edge of the Marimekko fabric. In March 1979, a major retrospective exhibition of Maija's work was organized at an art gallery in Helsinki. As many as 160 works, including her paintings and gouache sketches, were shown during the exhibition, though none of her textile designs were displayed. She eventually settled down in Finland.

Draft of *Kettulaakso*

Kettulaakso, 1979

Triangles inspired many designs in 1980. Right: the original sketches

Jojo, 1980

Sisilisko, 1981

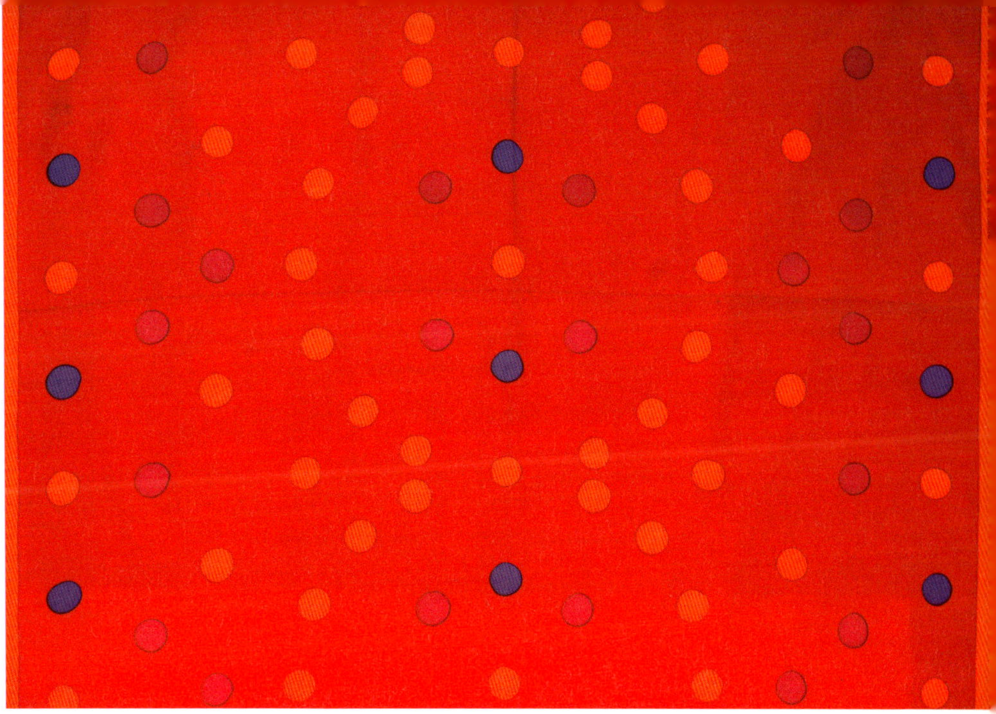

Pom-pom, 1982

Pata, 1982

Helmet, 1982

Hohtava, 1984

Ikaros, 1983

Visentti, 1984

Mother and daughter working together

The collaboration between Maija and Kristina was positive and productive. They went on trips to Paris together and other places in Europe for developing their ideas. During the winter, they worked at Maija's house in Helsinki, in Kaunismäki in the summer. They painted the final version of the print screen to preserve the original touch and feeling. Working hours were from 9 a.m. to 4 p.m., and after that they went on a walk and discussed their ideas for the next day. They usually worked on the same common themes, though they drew and painted in their own studio. In the 1980s, they increasingly designed prints for ready-made products like tablecloths, bed linens, and scarves. They also designed prints for clothing. Once Marimekko had bought a pattern, they came up with a name for the pattern. It was a fun game of association, where they took turns and said what popped into their mind. A positive attitude toward work was what Maija had learnt from the games she played with her sisters as a child.

In Boone, April 19, 1977.

Rehevä kasvi, 1977.7.27

Rehevä kasvi 1977, in Madison, Wisconsin, acrylic on canvas, 110x130 cm. Private collection. Photo: Markus Leppo

In 2008, with help from Kristina and Emma, a print design was made based on this painting. Drawings were prepared for the screen in advance.

Salaisuus, 1986

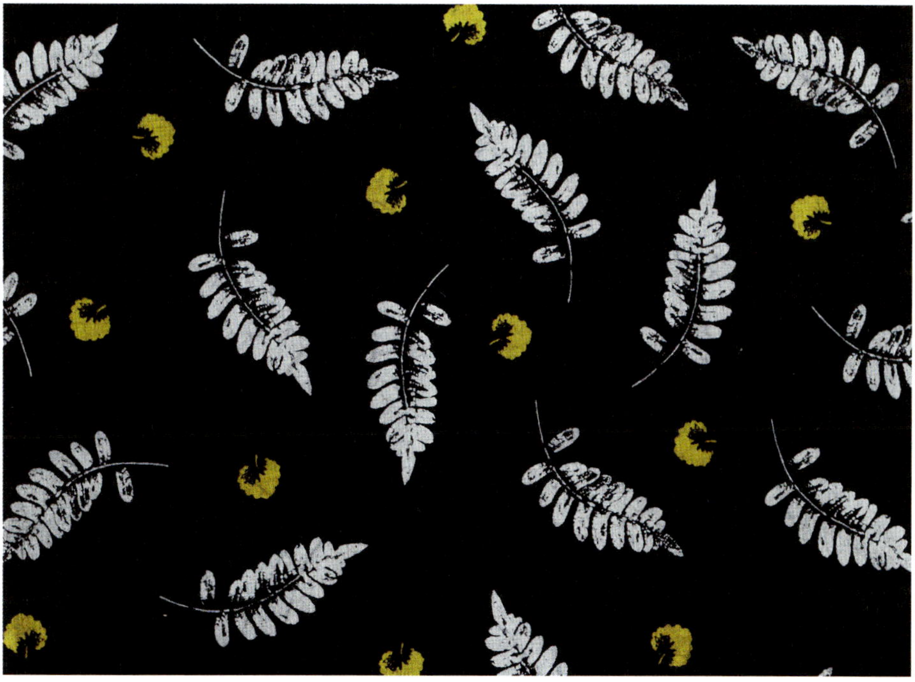

Aho, 1986

The late 1980s
– retirement and life in the forest

In 1987, Maija worked as a designer for Marimekko for the last time. Maija started to prepare for a new life and renovated the studio in Kaunismäki. She changed the place of some windows because she thought that the window was like a painting on a wall. Every time Kristina visited Maija, she informed her mother in advance. Kristina wanted to respect Maija's desire to be alone and she felt that it was the right thing to do. Maija's diary chronicles her life at that time. She took care of the garden and the surrounding woods, shoveled snow, baked bread, read books and magazines, listened to the radio, watched TV, and painted when she felt like it. She lived a quiet life.

Kristina continued to work as a designer for Marimekko. Besides her own designs, she was in charge of the rights for the design archive of Maija Isola. Maija's designs were almost forgotten until 1991 when Kirsti Paakkanen became Marimekko's CEO. Kirsti fell in love with *Fandango* and she decided to reproduce this pattern for the Christmas collection. Kirsti's foresight proved to be accurate and *Fandango* was a hit. Kirsti sent Maija a royalty check, but Maija returned the check with a letter.

November 27, 1992
Dear Kirsti Paakkanen,

I am so in love with the life in the forest here that I cannot accept any gifts. Thank you for the beautiful thought. I believe that you know better use for your money than I do.

Winter greetings from Maija Isola

Fandango, 1962

A legacy of patterns

In the late 1990s, Marimekko patterns became popular again. Hilkka Rahikainen, the artistic director of Marimekko at that time, decided to introduce a new type of textile collection and named it "Maija Isola Classic Collection." All the designs in this collection were based on Maija's textile patterns from the 1960s, except for *Kivet* and *Isot Kivet* from the 1950s. Colorways were loyal to the original designs. Maija experienced the great success of this collection. Maija used to mention the importance of creating an archive of her design work, because she was aware of the value of her works.

Illalla, 1988

Illalla 1988, oil on canvas.

Eternal journey

In September 2000, Maija learned that she was terminally ill. After a short stay in the hospital, Maija decided to spend her final time at home. Kristina, her daughter Emma and Maija's friends took care of her in turn. Maija calmly and patiently faced her own mortality. Maija passed away quietly in Kaunismäki surrounded by Kristina, Emma and Immi, Emma's two-year-old daughter, on March 3, 2001. It was a beautiful winter day. Kristina looked out the window and saw glimmering snow gently fall from the spruce trees. Then Immi said, "Maija has gone in her own way. She looks excited. Look, she is flying now." Maija Isola was a beloved designer, artist and mother. Her work will live on in the heart and imagination of people around the world.

Maija in Kaunismäki in the late 1990s.

Metsä, 1987

Kristina Isola

Maija's designs were hidden from the general public until the beginning of the 1990s. Later in the 1990s, vintage fabrics started to appear in window displays in the US and Japan. This global phenomenon inspired the production of the Maija Isola Classic Collection.

Ever since Kristina was a small child, she had grown up watching her mother work almost night and day. When Kristina visited Maija's house in Helsinki, she often went to the Marimekko factory with her mother. They would also drop by the Marimekko boutique. She still remembers how she was awestruck when she saw the colorful fabrics that were made from Maija's sketches.

Maija and Kristina often talked about textile patterns, and Maija always listened to Kristina's opinions. After Maija retired in 1987, Kristina became responsible for her mother's design legacy, while at the same time working on her own design work. In 2007, Kristina's daughter, Emma, become the third generation of Isolas to work as a textile designer. Soon Kristina will retire, and Emma will play an even bigger role in making sure the Isola legacy is passed onto future generations. "In order to follow in the footsteps of Maija, I would like to teach Emma as much as possible concerning our work," says Kristina.

Interview

Picture from *Marimekko Phenomenon* (1986).

Marja Hinttula

Marja started her career at Marimekko in 1964. Until her retirement in 2008, she worked as a shop manager, a product manager, a collection coordinator, and artistic director of the interior department. Marimekko has developed over the years, but the core part of Marimekko has remained the same. Marja was known for her honest feedback and was trusted by many designers. When she was working as a coordinator for Marimekko's interior design department, Marja had an opportunity to work with Maija Isola. She showed an old picture of Maija taken at Maija's flat in Kruununhaka. Everyone is sitting down on the floor and talking about the colorways of the scarf.

Maija's house was extremely minimalistic, according to Marja. When choosing colorways, Maija always tried to find the best combination;

she cut pictures of St. Petersburg and Tokyo from fine art books, showed the color chart that she painted by herself, and brought a ceramic dog. Marja was surprised when Maija started to cut clippings from the art book. Working with Maija was always full of energy and fun. Maija preferred to work alone, but during the production process, she discussed matters with Marimekko and showed an interest in the marketing and sales of fabrics. She rarely participated in the events organized by the company and gave an impression that she was difficult to approach. Marja looked back and said: "Maija was a very honest and natural person. She believed in herself and worked with great discipline."

Puu kuutamossa, 1977

Sami Ruotsalainen

Sami learned about Maija Isola when he joined the preparation for the exhibition of Maija Isola held in 2005. Although Maija had organized her archives very well, it was not easy to deal with the large amount of slides, diaries and pictures. Sometimes the work continued until midnight. Besides putting together the archive, he participated in every process: reproducing about 10 pieces of Maija's old designs and making the book. Throughout the year, Sami was deeply involved in the works, life and world of Maija. "I never met Maija but my understanding of Maija became deeper because Kristina shared many memories of her mother." Sami found that there are many similarities between Maija and Kristina in how they work. They enjoy following a certain routine and chatting during the work is prohibited.

"I do not know what to answer when people ask me what is my favorite print design by Maija. There are too many wonderful designs...," says Sami. One of his favorite fabrics is *Puu kuutamossa* from 1977. The design is based on a painting made in the US – a big tree shining under the moonlight. Kristina prepared beautiful colorways using light pink as a background. It was exactly the same scenery that he saw from the window of metro one day. And every time he sees a beautiful sunset, he thinks about this work.

Immi Isola

Anna Isola

Oliver Leppo

Frida Leppo

Saaga-Illuusia Luoto

Peppi Kalilainen

Osku

Maija Isola

2012 年 11 月 10 日　初版第 1 刷発行

Cooperation:	Kristina Isola, Emma Isola クリスティーナ・イソラ、エンマ・イソラ
Text & translation:	Eri Shimatsuka 島塚絵里
Photo:	Nao Shimizu 清水奈緒
Book Design:	Sachie Omori　(SMILE D.C.) オオモリサチエ
Editor:	Kaoru Takahashi 高橋かおる
Model:	Peppi Kalilainen, Immi Isola, Anna Isola, Oliver Leppo, Frida Leppo, Saaga-Illuusia Luoto
Special Thanks:	Katja Luoto, Satu Kallio

発行元	パイ インターナショナル 〒170-0005　東京都豊島区南大塚 2-32-4 TEL 03-3944-3981　FAX 03-5395-4830 sales@pie.co.jp

PIE International Inc.
2-32-4 Minami-Otsuka, Toshima-ku, Tokyo 170-0005 JAPAN
sales@pie.co.jp

編集・制作	PIE BOOKS
印刷・製本	図書印刷株式会社

Bibliography

- Maija Isola, Designmuseo, 2005
- In Patterns Marimekko, WSOY, 2012

Textile Index

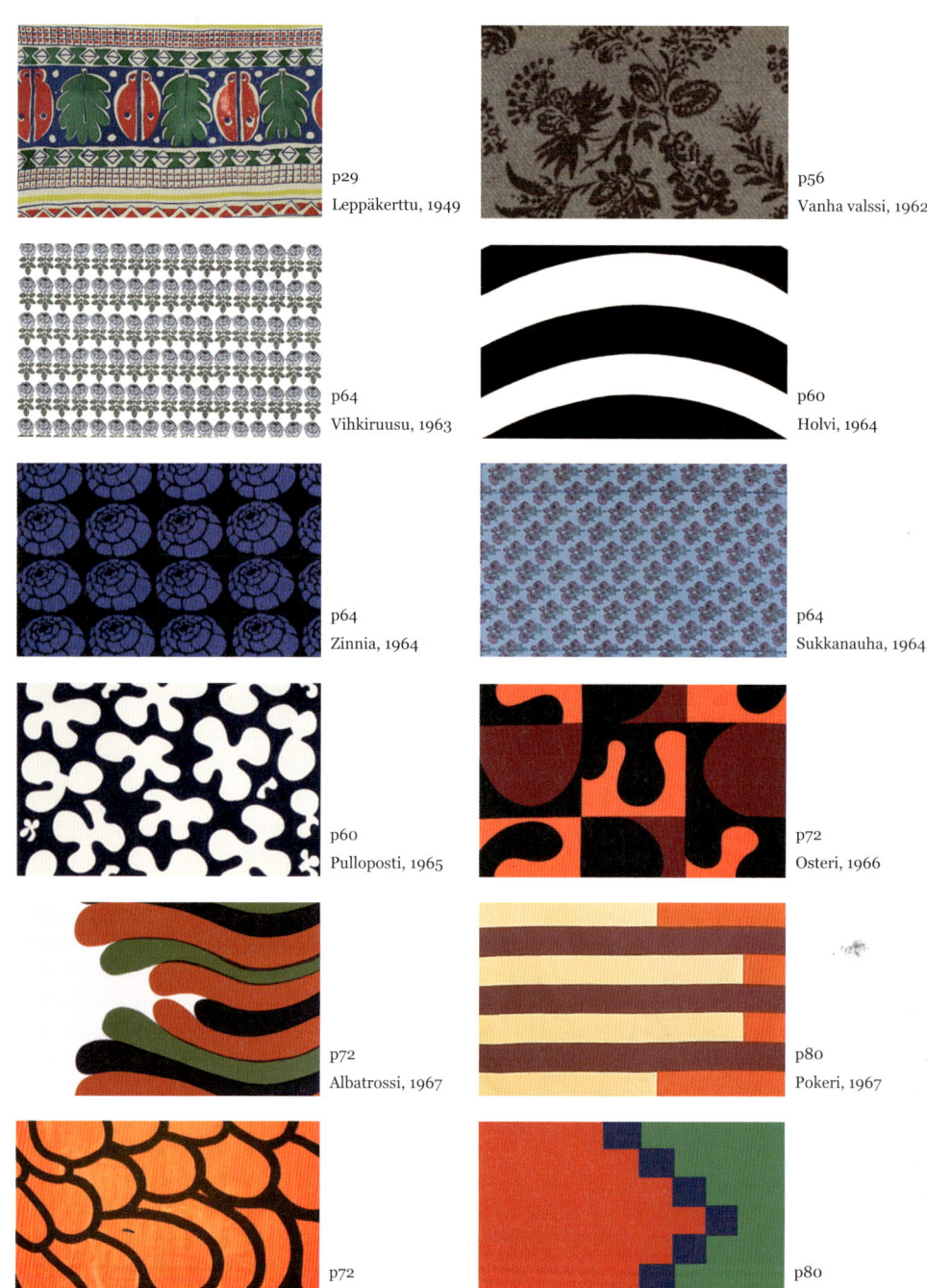

p29
Leppäkerttu, 1949

p56
Vanha valssi, 1962

p64
Vihkiruusu, 1963

p60
Holvi, 1964

p64
Zinnia, 1964

p64
Sukkanauha, 1964

p60
Pulloposti, 1965

p72
Osteri, 1966

p72
Albatrossi, 1967

p80
Pokeri, 1967

p72
Viikuna, 1967

p80
Musta Pekka, 1967